# Mari Nalu

# Mia and Christmas Snow

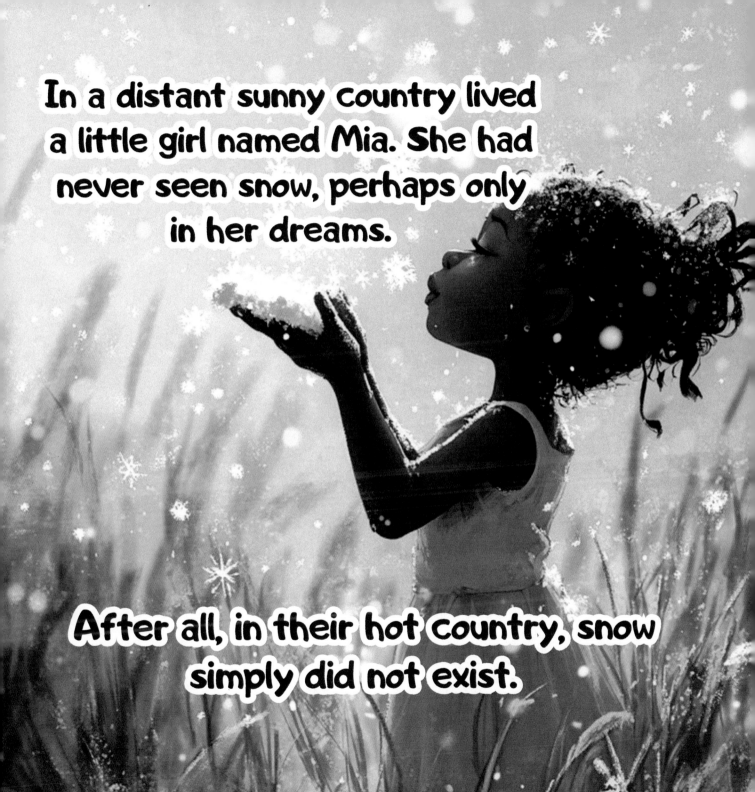

In a distant sunny country lived a little girl named Mia. She had never seen snow, perhaps only in her dreams.

After all, in their hot country, snow simply did not exist.

Mia's family had long planned to move to another country and start a new life, and it turned out to be a country where it snowed every winter. Mia was both excited and anxious about this big change.

As winter approached, Mia could not contain her excitement about experiencing a real Christmas with snow for the first time. She often looked out the window, imagining snowflakes falling softly from the sky and covering the ground with a white blanket.

The small town where Mia's family settled was decorated with lights and beautiful Christmas trees on the streets. Everywhere smelled of holiday spirit.

On Christmas Eve, Mia could not sleep from excitement. She crept to the window and saw that the first snowflakes had begun to fall. She ran out onto the street, feeling the cold air on her face, and watched in amazement as the snowflakes danced around her.

Suddenly, a small magical snowflake fell into Mia's palm. It sparkled and twinkled, filling her heart with joy. Mia whispered her Christmas wish to the snowflake, hoping it would come true.

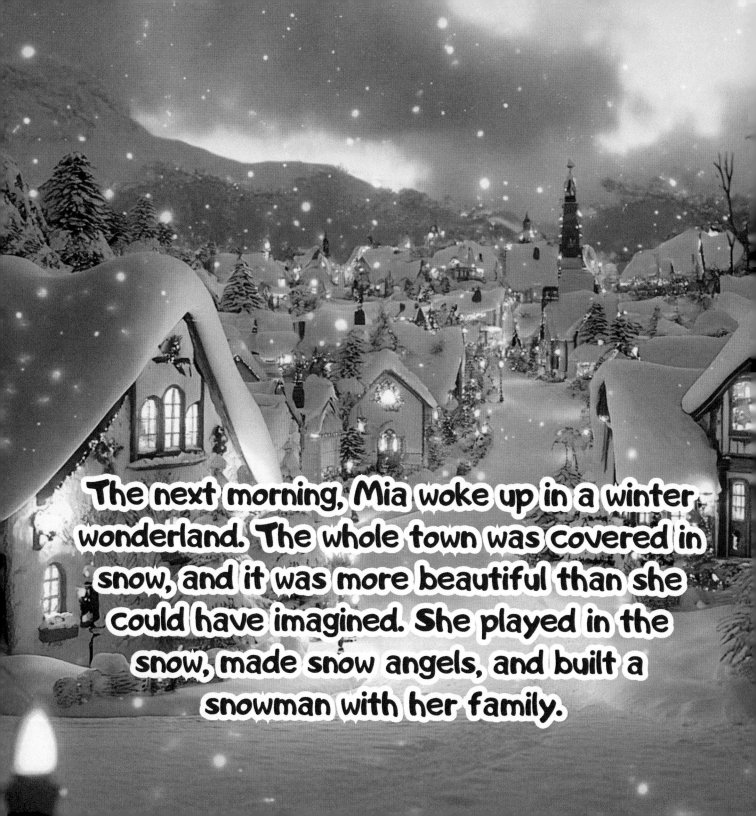

The next morning, Mia woke up in a winter wonderland. The whole town was covered in snow, and it was more beautiful than she could have imagined. She played in the snow, made snow angels, and built a snowman with her family.

There were other children having fun around, and Mia made friends with them. They shared their sleds and pulled Mia through the snow.

Looking up at the sky, Mia saw the same magical snowflake from the night before, sparkling and shining brightly. She knew her wish had come true, and she was grateful for this special Christmas gift.

From that day on, every time Mia saw a snowflake, she remembered that magical Christmas when she first experienced the beauty of snow.

And she knew that no matter where life took her, the memory of that special moment would always warm her heart. And the little magical snowflake continued to fall into the palms of those who sincerely rejoiced in the snow and the beauty of snowflakes.

After all, each snowflake is different, and there is not even one that is the same.

Amazing!

 if you want coloring me

if you want coloring me

if you want coloring me

Made in the USA
Las Vegas, NV
06 December 2024

13471755R00024